Excerpts From My Journal

by
Sarai Nichole

to the selves i've been—
i wrote this so you could rest.

©2025 Sarai Nichole

All rights reserved. No part of this publication may be reproduced, distributed, or transmitted in any form or by any means—including photocopying, recording, or other electronic or mechanical methods—without the prior written permission from the author, except for brief quotations used in reviews and or permitted by copyright law.

First Edition, 2025

ISBN: 978-1-0691332-0-5

Edited by Victoria Noon, Nichole Pedlar, and Joshua Macleod

Published by Sarai Nichole

Library and Archives Canada Cataloguing in Publication Data available upon request.

Printed in Canada

For inquiries or permissions, contact: sarainicholepoetry@gmail.com

Trigger Warning

This book contains discussions and depictions of mental health struggles, including suicidal ideation, anxiety, depression, ADHD, OCD, and intrusive dark thoughts. Reader discretion is advised.

If you find any of these topics distressing, please take care of yourself and step away if needed.

Proceed with care.

Dear Reader,

In these words, I found fragments of myself. If you too, find echoes of yourself within these pages, then we have truly met. May these entries greet you wherever you are and lead you to wherever you wish to go.

excerpts from my journal

they say we're too young
to know real heartbreak,
to experience real pain.
unfortunately, for us—

grief knows no age limits.

and sorrow fails to decipher the tenderness
of the bones it seeps so deeply into.
the anxious mind
does not consider the body it belongs to,
and love?

well—
love is the most selfish of all.

sarai nichole

to speak or to die—

to grieve all
that you didn't have the courage to say.
to allow someone to exit your life,
with an image
of you they have painted,
that lacks any depth at all.

now you feel somewhat
like a widow,
being abandoned
by the one they love.

are you still allowed
to consider yourself a widow,
if the person that left
did not know just how much they were loved?

excerpts from my journal

the other day,
i asked my best friend
what it feels like for her to fall in love.
she told me she wouldn't know—

she had never been in love.
and suddenly,
my wounds felt a little lighter.

because even though i have suffered
at the hands of love,
i have loved, nonetheless.

she turned the question back to me.
i told her i had become an expert
at recognizing my feelings,
because when i love someone—
when i let myself fall,
i become nothing but the love i have to give.

i wake up thinking about what it'd be like
to lie beside to them in the morning,
then i go to sleep early,
so our next moment together
doesn't feel so far away.

it's only when i don't feel
 completely consumed,
by the presence of another—
that i know i'm not in love.

we couldn't decide which was worse;
to only know all-consuming love—
even at your own expense—
or to never have your feet leave the ground.

sarai nichole

do not confuse love with infatuation.

it's one thing to daydream about them,
to miss them
the second they leave the room,
to feel as if you've known them forever,
and to want to tell them everything about yourself

as if it was your God-given purpose.

it's okay to feel admiration,
to want to show them off to everyone you know,
to wish they'd never leave your side.

but make sure you see them when they're angry.

when they've had a bad day,
and watch where they aim it.
see them sick,
breathing through only one nostril,
when their snores keep you awake
later than planned.

excerpts from my journal

notice them vulnerable,
when they ought to ask for help—
do they?

are they kind to strangers?
do they call their mother?
how often?
are you celebrated,
for the big things and the small?

do they talk about a future
that has you in it?
do they say, "i love you,"
and better yet,
do you feel loved?

it's one thing to dream
about all the ways they present themselves,

but will you still love them in a light,
they do not wish to be seen under?

sarai nichole

in the home of my grandparents, i lay parts of myself to rest.

in the muskoka room, the one that faces the backyard,
i let my grandfather's presence linger
in his designated chair.
a vision of rosy cheeks and laughter so deep
he'd be forced to remove his glasses, comes to mind.
nobody has dared to occupy that chair since.

sometimes,
when i find myself entranced by the haunting silence
of the woods surrounding their property,
i swear i can still hear the whispered giggles
erupting from the full bellies
belonging to my cousins and i.

up the gravel-filled driveway,
where beams of wood lay,
i balanced my two left feet
time and time again.

entering the foyer,
to your left is the kitchen.
pots and pans sway from above,
and the fridge still serves its purpose
of securing my grandmother's to-do list.

it's funny, though—
the fridge doesn't look quite as inviting
now that i can actually see over it.

you may notice the bite marks on the steps
leading to the living room.
yet all i can see
are the last traces of their golden retriever;
the stairs will remain brittle,
gnawed at and bare.

a part of me lays to rest with him, too.

the back hallway leads to two rooms,
forced apart by a hall closet
holding extra pillows and blankets
in case we ever needed them.
we never did.

our body heat never let us down.
found buried in the pull-out couch
that my cousin and i always preferred,
over the perfectly made bed
in the room across the hall.

when we were kids
we had ourselves convinced that room was haunted,
even though the bed in there
was undeniably the more comfortable option—
especially when compared to the couch
with one too many springs.

these days, i opt for the bed that's still perfectly made,
my back no longer what it used to be.

with walls too green and a rocking chair
that i swear still moves even with no life in it,

holding on to the few reminders,
that this house was once a home.

sarai nichole

people tend to assume
that the tattoos that decorate my body,
hold a significance too deep to be anything other than art.

i used to disagree.

my first tattoo, the word *family*,
in random cursive writing
high up on my wrist. i was sixteen.
cheesy to some, everything to those it honored.

a couple tattoos later and i was seated
in the basement of an artist who was recommended
by a friend, of a friend.
i was still sixteen, getting a matching tattoo
with my best friend, at the time.

we are no longer best friends,
but now the best parts of her
are embedded within my skin.
i prefer us that way.

when i asked my artist to give me a
crying cherub on my shoulder,
and she asked me if it had any meaning.
i told her that even the most beautiful,
sacred of things fall apart every now and then.

excerpts from my journal

when i got a silly tattoo of a ghost,
i thought to myself:
finally, *a tattoo just because.*
it held nothing but innocence.
ironically enough,
a year later,
i found myself adopting a dog.

the owner
had already given him a name,
—ghost.

and so, each tattoo stitched its way into my skin
as time carved meaning
where i thought there was none.
like the single-lined wave,
hidden beneath my under-arm,
reminding me this too shall pass.

or the snake on my upper thigh, which i swore
was just to keep me cautious,
that now whispered to me in quiet moments:
"shed what no longer serves you. let go, start again."

people still assume these inked
fragments of me are just symbols,
words, and pictures,
etched in deep significance,

a personal gallery of art—

i no longer disagreed.

sarai nichole

there is a great chance in your last moments,
you will be reliving everything you've done,
rather than the things you didn't do.

so, no matter how much—
or how little you do,
make it count.

excerpts from my journal

my fingers remain permanently curled,
the phantom grip of the suitcase handle
i refused to release,
exposing the longing that still lays with guilt,

i did it, mom—
just like you said i could,
just as you feared.
i was given my wings,
and i did not look back.

but you never told me when to stop flying,
never warned me that altitude
distorts the shape
of what i once called home.
i have touched down in places
where laughter sounds like our kitchen,
where the streets wear a perfume
i could swear i knew as a child—
and yet, when i return,
nothing fits where i left it.

i have gathered new ghosts.
the sun-drunk strays in corfu,
forgotten by a city
that forgot how to blink.
the sundays in heidelberg,
so still—
i could hear my own breath.
a silence that sang me lullabies.

sarai nichole

i am homesick for places
where my name is a question,
where my accent is an echo
of something half-formed, half-lost.
where i am only as rooted
as the fading footprints
i leave in train stations,
airport terminals,
hotel rooms that forget me as soon as i leave.

and yet,
if you asked me where home is,
i would still say your name.
because no matter how far i go,
no matter how many skies
i strain my neck to catch,
home will always be the arms that envelop me
with the same force,
no matter how much time has passed.

but tell me, mom—
what happens when i return
and the walls no longer recognize me?
when the rooms are smaller,
when the air is heavier,
when i search for the girl who left
and only find the woman
who has seen too much?

i did it, mom—
i soared.
and now,
i do not know how to land.

excerpts from my journal

we crossed paths one afternoon in may,
when she came to tour the dorms,
her room was next to mine.

i was rushing to catch a bus,
her friend was calling for my attention,
but all i managed was a half-smile,
not knowing enough german to respond.

the next time i noticed her,
through the walls—
frank ocean drifting softly into my room,
and for the first time,
i slept undisturbed.

i wish i could tell you how it all unfolded,
but i only know that one day
she was a stranger, and the next;

we were on the back patio above the garden.
her laugh as warm as the cheap rosé
we picked up from the grocery store that afternoon.

frank ocean played again,
her phone balanced on the ledge,
and i should stop here—
some things are best kept untouched,
but if by chance,
she discovers herself written within these pages,

know you'll always be my favorite keepsake.

sarai nichole

every now and then,
i lie awake and wonder,

was his greatest act of love,
the admission he couldn't swallow,
bound by guilt?

or—

was my desperate plea for him to stay,
the clearest sign
that i had yet to love myself?

last night, my best friend
left her reading light on my pillow.
i hadn't even asked;
she just knew
i'd want to read before bed,
as always.

i've never felt more seen
than i do in the quiet of my friendships.

sarai nichole

"*bring back yearning,*"
i tell my best friend,
as *dead poet's society*
plays softly in the background.

yet when he tells me
i may be his favorite view—
aside from his mother and the ocean,
i feel myself shrink.

when will a love like this find me?
i think,
as i absorb every last word
of Just for the Summer's final pages,
by Abby Jimenez.

but as he confesses,
all the ways he wishes to celebrate me,
how he's never felt so seen,
held by a gaze he'd risk getting lost in—
two black holes
he should be careful of, but isn't—

guilt lays where goosebumps should rise.

excerpts from my journal

mom tells me it's because subconsciously—
i accept only the love i believe i deserve.
though i can't imagine
how i came to see myself as unworthy.

i wonder where i went wrong,
when i was once the girl,
who held a love so pure
that anyone who saw it believed.

a love that never outgrew its innocence,
two souls that must have searched lifetimes
for one another.

i've been searching
for its remnants ever since.
and no matter the passion,
or the genuine devotion—

i can't help but wonder what he'll make of me
when he realizes i am best adored as an idea,
a concept half-formed.

sarai nichole

my mother
always rooted for the underdog.

the apple must not fall far from the tree—
after all.
but while she could simply root,
i spread like ivy—
inevitably,
twisting around whatever light i could find,
adapting to every season,
every storm.

as though i couldn't help myself—
believing that if i could just show them
the glow that still lingers,
even through tangled vines,
my faith alone might be enough
to make them bloom.

i wonder if my mother roots for me, too;
i wonder if i am somebody's underdog.

excerpts from my journal

you know that voice—
that one that only appears
once it's no longer of any use.

like after an argument with someone you love,
when every reason you had to be angry
starts to blur together,
leaving you with nothing but a dry mouth.

but the voice—
it finds you in the shower, just before sleep,
or in dreams, both awake and dormant—
whispering all the things
you should've said,
ideas sharper than the originals.

i have this recurring scene in my mind.
i'll call it a scene because i can't decide
if it's a dream or a nightmare—

you come back for me
when i least expect it.

i'm out with friends,
the ones who took it harder than i did,
when it was all brought to light.

one grips my arm,
another spins me around,
as if shielding me from you
could undo what's already been done.

sarai nichole

but it wouldn't matter anyway—
i could be stripped of every sense and still,
i'd know you were there.

i tell them it's fine,
that i'm no longer the girl i used to be—
a plea, mostly to myself.

i march toward you,
anger surging like it never left,
rehearsing every way
i'll tell you off,
reclaim what you left broken.

and then you *look* at me.

and i swear you're reading the lines
as i say them silently.
that stupid, poor-boy pout of yours in place.
and with a sigh,
worth nearly a year's build-up,
all i can muster—

i missed you.

i wait for that voice to step in,
to remind me of all the ways you left me hollow.
but we both know—

i have always been fluent
in the language of your silence.

excerpts from my journal

my mother told me,

it took me a long time
to forgive him,
but i was tired of carrying
the weight of anger. i did it for me.

i scoffed.

her forgiveness never was hereditary—
a common absence among the lessons
we teach ourselves.
in twenty-two years of living,
the only trace of my father
that held steady—

his rage.

sarai nichole

she will never understand
why your pulse quickens
at the sharp edge of a raised voice,
why the weight of a curse
feels heavier on your skin than it does hers.

she won't know how to reach you
when your grief,
disguised as anger,
builds walls faster than she can tear them down.
she'll think your silence is distance,
not survival.
she'll mistake your need for space
as something personal.

and even if she learns you,
memorizes every scar and soft spot,
knows the map of your mind
better than i ever could—
she will still have to meet me first.
because before her,

it was just us.

two people who spoke a language
the world never bothered to learn.
who carved out a space
where softness was allowed,
where breaking was safe.
no matter how much time passes,
no matter who stands beside you now,
we will always know what it took to let each other in.

excerpts from my journal

i realize now—
i made this plan
to move far away, to forget you,
to busy my mind until my heart followed,
to fill every silence where you once were.

but this was never healing,
only the art of distraction.
if i truly wanted to mend,
i would have to sit with this,
even when it unsettled my soul.
i would need to accept that yes—

some days would ache like open wounds,
and on others,
when tears threatened,
i'd let them fall.

i'm grieving someone who's still breathing,
mourning the words i was too afraid to say—
to both you and myself.

sarai nichole

i wonder—
would it have changed anything?
if i had poured out my heart,
leaving our fate trembling in your hands,
what would it have looked like?
for better or for worse,
i'll never know.

but if i could go back,
i would tell you everything.
even if you said nothing,
even if we never spoke again.

because life keeps breathing into others,
with or without you,
because people move on.

so now, i will sit with this ache,
let it take up space,
and learn to make peace
with all i'll (n)ever know.

excerpts from my journal

i have never been one to sink.
even in the heaviest moments,
i stay just above the undertow,
held up by the curse of knowing better.

it stops me from falling for potential—
but it also stops me from falling at all.
always hovering just above the surface,
skimming the edges of what could have been,
never lost enough to drown,
never free enough to swim.

i used to envy the ones
who never had to unlearn softness,
who mistook the fall for flying,
who never questioned
whether the ground was waiting.

there was a time i wanted that, too.
not because it was easy—
but because it wasn't.

to hand myself over to
something bigger than the life
i had so carefully curated.
to surrender without calculation,
without knowing the ending.

sarai nichole

but self-awareness
does not allow surrender.
it asks for clarity, for reason.
it keeps me safe—
but safety is not the same as living.

you beg for peace,
but peace is the absence
of feeling.
you ask for quiet,
but your mind will always be too loud.

and in the end,
it's not the noise that breaks you—
it's knowing exactly why
you'll never let yourself
be broken.

not again.

and even as we drift to sleep,
anger unshed and words unheard,
he reaches for me all the same—
fingers grasping at my thin tank top,
knowing no fabric could rival
my unwavering longing for his envelop.

reassurance marking its territory,
even his unconscious mind,
always reaches back for me.

sarai nichole

i am never still,
because even stillness demands motion.
and when my hands lay quiet,
my mind dances in its own rhythm,
a pulse that outpaces the body it belongs to.

in the roll of an eye,
or the tick of a jaw,
a tick—
like a clock that never knows silence.

i put my hand under my chin,
then to my knee—
but now my chin is cold,
so back it goes.
my legs aren't aligned

so i move—

just inches to the left,
but now the armrest
applying pressure, unequally;
so i shift—
and there goes that *damn* clock again.

to start everything,
and finish nothing.
the mind hums,
like a room full of alarms,

except nothing ever really burns.

looking back on buried friendships
is always bittersweet.

like one day, after hanging out for days on end,
i walked out the door and just never went back.

even though i knew where they hid the dog treats,
and i attended her sister's graduation—
her wanting me there just as much as i wanted to be there.
we did all the stupid things teenagers do,
in good company.

i wonder if her room is still set up the same way,
or if she ever went back to school.
if she wanted more for herself,
and if she got it.
i wonder if she still does stupid teenager stuff,
just with someone else now. i'd hope so—
risks aren't as scary in good company.

i wonder if she got our tattoo removed,
or what she says when people ask about it.
i hope she forgives me,
and if she reads this,
i hope she knows i forgive her too.

all the stupid things teenagers do

sarai nichole

but what if this is all we get?
moments that vanish as quickly as they come,
people who stay just long enough to leave.

would you still give away all your days,
if you knew *just* how many were left?

life doesn't wait for readiness,
it moves forward with
or without your permission,
while quietly collecting
all the things you meant to savor.

excerpts from my journal

there is so much intimacy in smaller acts;
the extra water left in the kettle—
your midnight tea,
the fan on level two,
one arm tucked under your pillow.

or the start of your car, on mornings
with frostbitten windows—
you weren't made for winter.
it's the consideration,

the unspoken defaults of love.

sarai nichole

and maybe one day,
he will live up to the potential that you—
always saw within him.
but it is not your job
to hold his hand, along a journey
you were never meant to seek.

you must center yourself,
build rituals that heal, share your light,
listen to the wisdom of your body,
and confront the quiet corners of yourself.
the unknown is not a void, but a beginning.
everything—
either a lesson or a blessing,
both finding a purpose within your shape.

he lost someone
who never believed those that doubted her ability—
to hold enough love for them both.
and his failure to reciprocate,
was never a reflection of you—
only a projection of his avoidance,
of traumas you were never built to heal.

love yourself enough to release him,
and love him enough to teach—
the truest lessons often bloom,
in the silence of what is missing.

and always remain kind.

excerpts from my journal

i've recently come to realize
that so many of these pages
carry the weight of my mother's name,
her presence etched into almost every line,
as though she were merely my muse.

but to call her a muse
would diminish the quiet strength of a woman,
who offered unwavering kindness,
even on days when the world
seemed to have nothing more to give than cruelty.

when i was an angry teenager,
cloaked in frustration
and retreating into the solace of my unmade bed—
she would knock on our doors at the same time,
singing her all-too-familiar, cheerful tune.

without warning,
she'd let light flood in,
the blinds drawn wide open
despite our moans and groans,
our pleas for her to leave
and let the curtains fall back down.

but she never did—
she couldn't.
because my mother was the light,
a tireless smile worn even on her hardest days.
and though we rolled our eyes at her cheesy mantras
about tackling mondays with coffee and optimism,
or heard the hum of her footsteps
at 5 am, letting out the dogs—

we never imagined the world to be cruel,
not when she made it feel so warm, so inviting.

sarai nichole

she was tired, i'm sure,
but you would never know.

day after day,
she washed the dirty dishes, and sorted endless loads of laundry.
she wiped away the fingerprints from mirrors,
and opened her heart to a man who claimed to love her,

but watched as she carried the weight—
breadwinner, maid, chef, mother, father—
while he remained still,

his only identity—
a man she no longer recognized.

and in return,
we ate meals prepared with love;
dinner always ready around five-thirty.
our closets smelled of tide,
clothes hung neatly on matching hangers.
we stood before spotless mirrors,
never thinking to question their clarity
as we completed our once-overs
on school mornings.

and my sister—
she would never know the weight
of a father's love that did not always greet her.

so yes,
i will speak of her fondly,
with words that attempt to capture
a love that asks for nothing in return.

because my mother—
the most selfless woman
i have ever known—
allowed me to become
all that she could have been

excerpts from my journal

most people can't believe it
when i tell them i lived in a house *full* of girls
during university—
"sure, it's cheap, but imagine the lack of space!"
they say, wide-eyed.
and honestly, they're not wrong.

be prepared for those who wake up
four hours before you,
and those who always forget
to rinse the knives
before they go in the dishwasher.

yet no one warns you
of how quickly it becomes your world.
how comforting it is
to hear someone call your name
from the bottom of the stairs.

and then it's over.

you'll move back home
to a space you once longed for,
and it will feel unnervingly still.
quiet mornings,
your feet echoing against bare floors,
the absence of overlapping lives.

by day seven,
you'll wake up with the sun—
finally understanding how your roommate
found joy in the quiet hours:
the scent of coffee brewing,
the soft clatter of keys as she worked ahead,
pulling you into mornings
you never planned to greet.

sarai nichole

some nights,
you'll sit in the stillness,
and remember the exhaustion
you swore you'd never miss—
the whispered complaints during all-nighters,
the shared ache of sleepless eyes.
other nights, you'll recall how they stayed—
helping you carry the weight,
your feelings unraveling into theirs.

there will be a moment when the ache settles in,
sharp and sudden—
as you remember the rush of girlhood.
laughter pouring over countertops,
the chaos of too many mirrors,
of slick-backed hair and endless tube tops.
a different genre playing from each floor.

so, don't be too quick to leave it all behind—
at least not for the reasons they'll warn you about,
but because you'll miss the way it felt
to squeeze so much life into one house.
to be part of something so loud,
so full, so fleeting—

because no one tells you
how much smaller your world becomes
when it's just you,
in the quiet mornings.

you can enjoy being alone,
and still not want to be lonely.

excerpts from my journal

my best friend once worked at a coffee shop,
and God-
do i ever envy this woman.

"a breath of fresh air,"
my grandmother said, seconds after they met.

she moves through the world like it owes her nothing.
sets fire to what no longer serves her—
and never looks back.

yet somehow,
she still apologizes
for things that were never her fault.

she carries pain in silence,
never asks the world to slow down for her.
even when she should.

she once debated calling in sick,
afraid she couldn't meet the day's demands.
she paced, hesitated—
and then finally made the call.

"she wasn't even mad," she laughed,
"it's just coffee."

sarai nichole

as if everything heavy could be made light,
if only you let it.

and just like that, a new mantra was born.

my best friend makes me believe
life can be as simple
as i allow it to be.

she asks for rain,
and the world gives her storms.
yet somehow, she finds poetry in the flood.

you know those people,
the ones who make you feel
like you could do absolutely anything?
that's her.

and if the world refuses
to reflect her light back at her when she needs it most,
let it be me.

let it always be me.

excerpts from my journal

when i was a child,
elderly people frightened me—
even my own relatives.

i believe now,
it had less to do
with wrinkles and protruding veins,
and more with the silent knowing
of what was to come.

i failed to see past frail bones,
skeletal-like fingers,
to understand the true honor,
of witness love aging
before my very eyes.

cheekbones carved thin,
etched by years of sorrowful smiles.
hips softened and worn—
not just by the bearing of life,
but by small hands gripping tightly,
toddlers clinging for one too many years.

a back that bends, no longer standing tall,
once the throne for children,
their arms looping a neck,
legs wrapping a waist,
their laughter spinning the world in circles—
until stars danced behind closed eyes.

sarai nichole

my great-grandmother,
the only one i have left.
with her english accent
and cardigans in every color,
turns ninety-seven this spring,
her mind still decades behind her.

no longer able
to take me berry-picking,
her lap too fragile
to hold me
and all the books
she used to read aloud.

she is a force—
the woman who outlived her son
and her husband, too.

and while we all beamed selfishly
at each birthday she reached,
i wonder if my younger self
recognized the familiar ache of losing sight of those
who already lost sight of you.

excerpts from my journal

there is something so beautiful,
so *consuming*—
about watching strangers
go about their lives.

the elderly couple boarding the train,
hand in hand.
a husband still carrying
all the weight,
even if his wife could bear it.
she never needed to;
he never let her.
how many grandchildren, i wonder,
cried in their driveway,
waving as the car grew smaller?

the gas-station employee,
who welcomed everyone with a smile,
one rarely returned.
her kindness, unreciprocated,
a fragile offering left in the cold.
i always made sure to ask her
how her day had been.
did she ever whisper to herself at night,
hoping someone had noticed her trying?

the man who walks his dog
along the same weathered path each day—
i wonder who needed the walk more, dog or man?

sarai nichole

the young man always dressed
in outfits only *he* could compliment,
the only stagnant article he wore—
oversized headphones.
was he drowning out the world,
or escaping what could not be seen?

the new parents on the block,
the ones with a newborn so tiny,
neighbors pause mid-stride—
unable to resist the magnetic pull of new life.
whose name, i wonder,
did they choose to honor,
hidden within the child's initials?

there's beauty in the unspoken,
in the gaps we fill with our quiet hope.

perhaps that's what makes it all seem so beautiful.
the way we allow ourselves to believe there is good,
even without certainty.

as the older sister—
a part of me sympathized
with the teenager before me.
the one too proud to name her battles,
yet all too tired to fight them.

with blinds held shut, and curtains closed,
her room was always a shade too dark—
holding a silence that needed no company,
yet felt heavy in its own way.

at an age where boys turned crueler,
bodies began to change
and innocence became currency,
too easily spent.

the youngest of three generations,
with so much yet to learn
and too much to lose—
i met her with tenderness.

because bitterness stained my teenage years,
leaving scars that never fully healed.
my sister's wounds laying
as fresh as the present,
her skin still tender—

i couldn't shield her from what was to come,
but i could hold her hand,
and promise to be there
whenever she was ready to need me.

sarai nichole

we look for them in everything, don't we?

we suffocate as we steal their breath,
and we begin gasping for air,
in wind of their departure.

to love or not to love

excerpts from my journal

tomorrow marks two years
since you've been gone.
and not a day has passed,
that i don't reach for you,
longing for your steady presence.

even in death,
you remain honored.
in the middle name
of my unborn children,
incubating in my notes app.
children who will never know the privilege
of learning from a man,
with so much to teach.

sarai nichole

my grandfather—
the man he was—
taught me some of life's greatest lessons.
and even now,
in passing,
he reminds me
that love is not held in grief,
but in the breath we take,
for those who cannot.

so, i will carry his love
just as i always have.
and it shall sit with me,
in the spaces
we no longer get to share.

excerpts from my journal

i think i will visit my father on his death bed.
i will let him know that
forgiveness sends its regrets.
my only peace offering will be
the glimpse before him—
the woman i became in his absence,
the one i could have never been
had he stayed.

a proposed glimmer of hope,
just outside of arm's reach—
only for him to realize
there is no time left
to undo the damage,
to salvage all that has been lost.

only then will he come to understand

irony at its cruelest.

sarai nichole

dreams don't die;
they just narrow—
settling into the cracks
of who we are meant to become.

when my mother became a counsellor,
i thought, *i'll help people, too.*
when i was sixteen and in love,
i thought,
*i'll be the kind of mother my mother was—
steady, unshakeable.*
and when my best friend read my journal,
she said, *you're good at this. better than good.*
so i thought,
maybe i'll write something
the world would read someday.

i wanted to be everything—
to see the impossible as small,
to believe that even the quietest efforts matter;
to save lives no one else noticed slipping away.

and somehow—
i became everything i ever wanted to be.

i worked with the homeless
and sat in classrooms with those incarcerated,
who taught me more about resilience
than any textbook ever could.

excerpts from my journal

i wandered through german streets for months,
chasing shadows in cobblestone alleys,
watching the world expand
with every train i boarded.
i swam in waters that felt like promises
and wrote words that made me feel infinite.

i have lived so many lives already.
and maybe that's the secret—
you don't have to choose.
you don't have to do it all at once.
you only have to trust
that each will come when it's time.

i had people in my life who believed in me
long before i could.
who spoke my name with kindness
in rooms i'd never stepped foot in.
their faith spoke louder than my fear,
and their kindness reached further than my doubts.
they held the mirror steady,
until i could finally see myself in it.

and my mother— she told me i could, so i did.

the only thing between us and the life we want
is simply daring to believe it's yours.

find someone you believe in, and let them believe in you.

sarai nichole

it wasn't quite love at first sight,
at least not with us.

he was so quiet,
and all i had ever known
was how to be loud.

i moved with caution,
learning to tiptoe
through the stillness he called home,
afraid my noise might shatter his peace.

but in shrinking myself,
i discovered something profound—
that to love someone is to speak their language,
to offer your heart in ways they can hold.

so, i tried to meet him in the silence,
but even there, his head did not turn.
it wasn't disinterest;
he was simply listening for something else.

excerpts from my journal

though quiet was his sanctuary,
it was my noise that stirred him.
it was the chaos of my laughter,
the unfiltered honesty of my words,
the sound he had never dared to make,
that woke something dormant inside him.

and that's how he loved me back—
not by altering himself,
nor by meeting me halfway,
but by letting my voice fill the spaces his silence could never reach.

i found solace in the stillness he offered,
while he came alive in the storm of my presence.
it wasn't perfect, but it was pure—

a reminder that love doesn't require sameness,
only a willingness to let each other be heard.

sarai nichole

when it's two in the morning
and i'm everywhere i shouldn't be—
i wonder if you're doing the same.

i wonder if your finger hovers
over the familiar symbol on your screen—
and then,
i wonder if i still hold a contact name.
do your friends spur you on?
or do they remind you that you are not able to
fall back into old patterns,
faultless?

the only customary habit
we always shared,
the addiction gene.

i don't tell my friends,
because then i'd be forced into acknowledgement.
painfully reminded that healing
is less linear than i'd imagined it to be.
that i hadn't come as far as i'd hoped,
at least not yet.
but you won't call,
and i wouldn't answer anyways—
that's exactly how it should be.

you should know what that's like,
to mask manipulation as a mistake,
a bad habit you *promise* to get ahold of.

i always notice the moon peering through my curtains,
during the hours i allow you to haunt me—
and i know it sees me too.

excerpts from my journal

my best friend and i rarely hugged,
but when we did,
it always felt sort of like
an apology.

like the release of a breath,
contrasted by the clench of a jaw.
two souls speaking in every way
except outwardly—

"i'm so sorry we did not grow up on the same street.
i'm sorry that i wasn't there
to follow you through the playground,
squeezing us both into one slide
until our hip bones were practically conjoined.
and i'm sorry i never got to tell you
that i too, had an angry man in my house—"

even with the highest odds
of not being able to save one another,
we would've tried anyways.

i believe we could've been
as brave as we were today.

sarai nichole

the first time i learned
that dogs couldn't eat chocolate,
i was in the fifth grade.
a classmate told us about a little girl
who tried to feed her yorkie,
chocolate.
i didn't understand why she was so upset,
so i went home and asked my mother.
she told me chocolate is poison for dogs.

i hated the world for it.

when it was your turn,
i opted for a cheeseburgers instead
—extra bacon.
two of them, because i knew
you'd scarf the first one down
and still look for more.
i watched you eat,
tears streaming down my face.
your eyes looked just like mine,
glossy and tired.
i told myself it was just old age,
because thinking you knew this was goodbye
was too much to handle.

we went home and mom had us sit on the stairs,
for a final family picture.
her smile was bright,
her face red from crying.
she was being our mom, like always—
making sure we had what we needed,
even while losing her best friend.

excerpts from my journal

at the vet,
they brought you a chocolate sundae.
your tail wagged weakly,
one last time.

by the time mom leaned down to you,
your body couldn't move anymore.
in that moment,
she wasn't just our mom.
she was a little girl,
broken and crying for her best friend,
and there was no one left
to lick her tears away.

that was the first time i saw my stepdad cry,
he couldn't look at us, he never went inside.
i sat there, so angry at the world,
just as i did all those years ago—
angry at the universe,
angry that love could feel this cruel,
angry that we had to let you go.

and in the silence that followed,
the world felt so empty,
as if it, too,
mourned you.

sarai nichole

daddy's little girl

but just for a moment—
i imagine he is not my father.
not the man who helped me
wash the family car as a child,
held me high on his shoulders at the zoo,
or carried me inside when i fell asleep on the ride home.

he is not the man who stopped showing up
when i asked for more than he could give—
when i asked him to still be a father,
even though i was no longer his little girl.

instead, i see a man sitting alone
at the kitchen table,
a frozen meal thawing beneath tired hands.
after a long day's work,
he walks through halls
emptied of the footsteps
he once grew tired of hearing.

i imagine him checking his phone one last time,
scrolling through unreturned messages,
before sinking into an unmade bed
where silence greets him like an old friend.

"but the phone works both ways,"
he might say—
yet somehow, i know,
it is easier to be lonely
than it is to be a father.

sometimes,
our only purpose is to be—
to exist as we are,
without apology or pretense.

the moment you surrender
to the raw truth of yourself,
when you embrace every fractured,
yearning, and radiant part of your being—
you will move through the world
with the quiet power of someone
who is wholly unshaken.

sarai nichole

oh darling,
don't you get it?
you *are* good.
the fact that you lose sleep,
wondering if it will ever be enough,
is proof that it already is.

the inherently bad do not linger
on questions of goodness—
they do not ache to be better.

the victim complex

to wrap yourself in solitude,
the quiet companionship of a teacup and a cat,
convincing yourself that pushing away all you knew
is the dawn of something in bloom—
and not the slow fade of the credits.

or—

to forgive.
when the choice stands before you—
to forgive or to resent—
i hope you find it within yourself to forgive.

you'd be shocked to discover
how different your life might have been,
if those around you
had chosen violence over grace.
forgiving you for the faults you could not see.

no one is asking you
to let it all go,
that is no answer, either.
we are only here to remind you,

that you can always be more
than what happened to you.

sarai nichole

i believe that love gets sweeter as you age,
yet i can't seem to decipher exactly what it is.

i had the privilege
of watching my mother
fall into different versions of love.
and i call this a privilege
because had the stars not aligned
exactly as they did,
i wouldn't have been able to trust
that love will find me at each age i come to be.

love in your twenties is exhilarating.
it is dramatic,
and it is painful.
it comes with many firsts,
followed by many lasts.

it is the in-between
of becoming everyone you have ever been,
and those who you will come to meet.

love in your thirties is grounding,
but in the settling sense.
feeling so far
from adolescence,
but retirement falling nowhere in sight.

excerpts from my journal

the fear of this being
all you get and the hope
that one day
it might just be enough.

love in your forties
is an unconscious habit,
as it should be.
how could you *not* be full of love and hope,
when your heart has endured
forty years of experience?
this love is soft, genuine, and considerate.

it's the lessons learned
through blended parenting
and the budding romance
of your dogs.
it is the hidden intimacy—
a passionate grasp
of hips that have birthed,
hobbies that went from pub crawls
to sunday golf, and nine o'clock
becomes the scheduled time
for netflix,
with extra pillow talking.

there is no simple,
one-size-fits-all answer,
to the preservation of love.
all i know
is that somewhere between the decades,
i remembered why children yearn to grow up.

sarai nichole

they will never know
just how much anger it took for you to be this still.

to sit in the heat of your wounds,
invite them for coffee,
and hear their grievances without flinching.
to learn they were never meant
to be your soulmates—
just the kind of guests who overstay.

you invited your pain to speak—
to tell its stories,
to show you the depths
of what you've survived.
it demanded acknowledgment,
not control,
and you met it halfway.
you let it bleed its truth,
but never let it drown you.

it takes years to learn
that peace is not a prize
for those who never fell apart.

excerpts from my journal

it is the moment you stop offering your rage
a hand in waiting.

it is the realization
that you are no longer the battlefield,
but the survivor standing
among the ruins, breathing—
promising—
that you will rise,
even as they wager on your fall,
even as the weight of the past tries to anchor you.

to be still is not to surrender—
it is the quiet defiance
of a heart that refuses to be sacrificed,
once more.

sarai nichole

you forgot your leftovers in my fridge
and each time i reach for the handle,
i am reminded of what you've left behind.

my family keeps asking me
what i would like done with them.

i don't know.

i suppose i could eat them,
but it wouldn't bring me the same joy
it always brought you.

every day that goes by,
they remain, as do i—
softening, turning,
holding on longer than they should.

excerpts from my journal

the problem is,
i'm not sure when you'll return,
if ever—
or if i can bear
ridding myself of the lasts of you.

you forgot your leftovers in my fridge,

and i fear
i would rather watch them rot,
let them sour and swell,
than replace them with something,
that does not offer a possibility
of your return.

sarai nichole

last week, a man i've deemed of high importance
told me that the most beautiful thing
for a woman to be—
is a mother.

that it was the most sacred of things,
anyone could offer this world—
the opportunity of existence.

and after careful reflection,
i concluded that his opinion
did not come from a place of ignorance,
yet of admiration.
i realized that we as humans tend to bear much significance,
upon the very things
we will *never* be able to offer this world.

i began to imagine the endless possibilities,
if only men had realized just how much *they*—
had to offer this very world.

the importance of being a father.

excerpts from my journal

imagine if the average man,
had valued the importance
of a child growing up with both parents,
present—
as much as they did,
the idea of a woman becoming a mother.

because just as there are things
a woman can offer a child
that a man could never;

i cannot show a boy how to be a man.
i can do my best to teach him,
to explain it in every way the female mind can—

but i will never be an honorable father,
for as long as i am a good mother.

sarai nichole

the man i loved the most
could not fathom a reasoning,
behind my instinct to flinch,
each time he offered his embrace.

i knew it offended him. it offended me too,
as i knew the truth—
i held no *subjective* reasoning to extend.

violence was never in the eye of the beholder;
it did not mirror a reflection upon my irises.

violence was in the hands of the man
meant to love me the most,
the one who should've loved me first.
and because of this—

i spared no grace to the palms of another.

the ocean— i replied,
when they asked me what i feared the most.

because no one ever seems to question
what the mind can easily rationalize.
a fear so vast it feels universal.
but deep, dark waters
did not shake me to my core.

it was the surrender.
the sacrifice of the woman i'd built,
brick by brick,
admission after admission,
from the ruins of shed skin.
i had shown no interest
in the game of russian roulette.
to love or not to love,
to be cradled or to be consumed?

and what if i could not find her again?
what if love demanded a version of me,
that the eyes of my being did not recognize,
or one i no longer yearned to become?

they say you cannot love deeply,
without offering each vessel of the heart.
but i ask them—
to what is the worth of a love
that asks you to vanish for its survival?

yet all i could muster,
was the familiar expanse of unknown waters.
because no one ever questions
a fear they can face.

sarai nichole

he exclaimed his love for me
from rooftops,
loud—
like a truth that couldn't be ignored.

disguised as a secret,
being held
between the lips of adolescence.
he spoke of me in ways
that could convince
almost anyone,
i had built the very ground he walked on.

but when we were face to face,
skin against skin,
within the walls we built together,
he couldn't find the words.

that's the thing about love,
it holds no weight if it cannot be reached
by the one person that gives it a purpose.

excerpts from my journal

some people live their whole lives
without ever knowing
the cost of understanding.

they will never wake up
with the weight of the world
lodged in their throat.
never feel truth press against their ribs
like something trying to break out.

there is equal beauty and tragedy
in the honesty of the world.

for every answer gained,
something is lost—
the quiet wonder,
the comfort of not knowing.

sarai nichole

be grateful that some questions remain unanswered.
to belong to a mind still curious
is to exist in a place
untouched by ruin.

to be intelligent,
is to grieve.

knowledge does not arrive gently.
it does not fold itself into you
like a whispered secret.

it burrows. it corrodes.
it makes a home
in the hollows of you and calls itself wisdom.

you must not prepare to memorize,
but to mourn.

excerpts from my journal

sibling to sibling
sister to sister...

for as long as i am breathing
you will always have a place in this world.
and in death,
i will find you again,
to remind you,
not a single moment passed
where you didn't make me proud.

i will find you in every lifetime to come,
because i made you a promise;
to protect you from monsters—
even those we can't see—
and to hold space for all your emotions,
big and small, even the ones i can't feel.

so, when i am laid to rest,
i dream not to be honored
as merely a lover,
a writer,
or a daughter,
but a *good* sister.
and if i am to one day be a mother,
my children, too,
will know i loved raising you first.

sarai nichole

they claim
it's not about what's outside,
but *it is*.
it's about the echoes of our laughter
rattling through thin summer air,
the trees we climbed
until the branches gave way,
scraping childhood into our skin.

it's about the forest behind us—
the one we weren't supposed to find,
where grasshoppers leapt from our hands
as if to remind us
that nothing stays still for long.
we chased each other
like we could outrun the lives
we weren't old enough to claim,
only to return to our separate homes,
to the secrets behind each door.

the girl behind me,
with dreams too big for our town,
became a flight attendant—
always meant for the clouds.
the girl next door,
separated by a crumbling wall,
found new people.
i hope they love her
half as much as we did.

excerpts from my journal

the girl across the street,
the one with a laugh
that could split open the dark,
lost her dog, then her father.
i pray she finds it in her to keep laughing.

even the bully down the road—
i pray for him too.
i pray his father's hands stopped leaving bruises
where a boy's innocence should have been.

now i see them through a screen,
their lives distant and pixelated.
we exist in separate worlds,
but sometimes i still feel the strings.

they tell you it's not about what's outside,
but *it is*.
it's about the windows thrown open
on buzzing summer nights,
just to catch the sound of us,
being the children of the block—
the children who made every minute count
because deep down, we knew.

life would never let us stay.

sarai nichole

the addiction gene

it greets you as innocence,
a decision made in a fleeting moment.
*a celebration, a death,
a farewell, or new life—*
cigars on the green,
a belmont in paris,
a singular glass of wine—
just for the edge.

that moment when
attention becomes a weakness,
and dependency buys you out.

some called them addicts.
i called them
*lovers,
fixers,*
those who didn't believe in evil
until they knelt before it.

aren't we all chasing something?
a high—
the rush—

nothing.
something.

anything.

excerpts from my journal

it's quite scary,
the way our ghosts
begin to haunt us so easily
we tend to forget they're present.
yet they demand to loom, nevertheless.

oftentimes,
it is the shackles
too debilitating to be imagined,
a figure of the mind.

i do not wish to be confined only to spaces i deem safe.

nor do i want to starve,
to linger,
to rot—
to only find light among the dark.

i do not wish to hide—

though i am only ever noticed in somber.

sarai nichole

may you never have to endure
the silence of lying awake
in an unmade bed,
holding your breathe
to ensure your sobs are not louder
than your heartbeat—
as the one you love
sleeps soundly beside you,
dreaming in a world where you do not exist.

you lie there,
counting the hours until dawn,
not for rest,
but to stretch time itself,
to live every stolen moment with them awake.
for the truth of love
is not the act of losing,
but the knowing

that morning always comes.

excerpts from my journal

but maybe
tomorrow will be better.

so, you live.
just until tomorrow.

sarai nichole

new year's resolutions

and when the clock strikes midnight
this new year's eve,
i will leave you behind;

for i have carried this grief long enough.

excerpts from my journal

you still love autumn,
but now you miss the way it smelled
when you were eight—
wet leaves and pumpkin pie.

you still watch the trees change,
only now the colors remind you
of just how much can be lost
in a single season.

sarai nichole

you can only sit and stare
at your wounds
for so long.

it will not make them heal faster,
nor erase their coloring.
whether your vision lingers on them
or wanders elsewhere,
it will not change their odds of bruising.
you will wince,
and still,

the sun will rise tomorrow.

healing is a process you'll never predict,
one that always carries the chance
of complications, inconveniences—
but the world will not stop.
it will not wait for you to catch up.

may this be more than just a poem about aching flesh.

excerpts from my journal

and eventually,
i would go on to love many others—

but still,

i'd whisper your name
beneath each uniquely shaped moon,
hoping that maybe,
just maybe—
you'd whisper mine too.

different stars,
always the same moon.

sarai nichole

everything i let go of
has claw marks on it,
yet my skin is still bare.

i bleed for the ones who threaten to leave,
begging, always begging,
as if my longing could anchor them—

but they never pause,
never falter at the edge.
their hands on my shoulders,
a gentle nudge disguised as care.

i've become fluent
in the language of departure—
in learning how to cling
while pretending to release.
every goodbye echoes,
and every echo feels like a hand
prying me apart.

everything i let go of has claw marks on it,
but no one ever notices
how my hands still tremble.

excerpts from my journal

they asked me why everything i wrote
was so sad,
so deep.

"because that's what the truth
about all of this really is.
it is sad, and it is deep," i replied.

"it's pathetic really—
filled with sorrow, corruption, betrayal.
we make friends just to lose them,
we fall in love
only to experience real pain.
we ache for what we don't know,
and we take for granted the rest.

my writing calms the mind,
because i have accepted what is true—
and i have chosen to make it beautiful,

everyone is sad,
so they pretend to have it all,
because their reality is not good enough.
i accept life for what it is—
overdone, unfair, and lacking depth.
yet my ability to feel it all,
for exactly what it is—
now that is beautiful."

sarai nichole

"do not borrow grief from the future"
but what if it offers misery in advance?

from the moment
you dropped me off at departures—
teary-eyed, swaying with impatience—
i knew grief
would be waiting for me at the gate.

those were not tears of sadness.
they filled eyes silently begging for forgiveness.
as they met my gaze,
they pleaded:
*"i cannot keep you,
no matter how badly you wish to stay."*

i did not borrow grief from the future;
it arrived early,
its shadow already leaning against the gate,
watching me leave,
and waiting to follow.

and i did not envy the girl,
though i couldn't offer her much pity either.
her gaze fixed on my knees,
straightening like a flag of surrender,
as she patiently waited to take my seat.

once, i too believed
in the soft alchemy of love,
thinking my hands could reshape
the jagged edges of his conscience,
carved by the wreckage
of a mother's trying love.

but every touch cut me deeper,
every whisper spilled promises
he had no intensions of keeping.

sarai nichole

now, outside his orbit,
the air tastes sweeter.
the quiet hum of my own heart
is louder than the chaos of his love.

i see her—
naivety draped like a velvet curtain;
her hands already bloodied
by the fight she doesn't yet know she'll lose.

and though i ache for her,
for the weight she's yet to carry,
i cannot envy her.
because i know the truth:

the man she holds in her dreams
is the ghost who haunts mine.

*"do you really need the person who hurt you
to tell you about the pain they've caused?"*

no,
i was never looking for an apology—
that would've been a waste,
especially from someone
lacking the emotional capacity,
to see their behavior
as more than
"the result of instigation."

i just wanted him to tell me the truth,
i could handle it, i really could.

what i could not accept
was the quivering lip of a coward,
spineless and steeped in so much deceit
he could no longer distinguish what was real.
i could not fathom
the greed for equal parts adulterine
and genuine connection.

but we do not ask for fish to fly,
so how could i ask a battered boy
for the spine of a man?

sarai nichole

no, we never did quite get it right.
but maybe in another life,
i'd be downstairs burning waffles,
since we both preferred them
much over pancakes.

and you'd be upstairs ignoring the kettle,
and we'd laugh about it later,
because none of it would matter.

the kids would be gone for the day,
at one in-law's or another,
and we'd waste the time together.

lighting candles for no reason,
folding sheets and crawling back into them,
letting the hours stretch long and easy
like the soft murmur of contentment.

excerpts from my journal

maybe in another life,
you'd press your hand to mine,
and it would mean more
than all the words
we never found the courage to say.

we'd still be us,
just softer,
just slower.

and that, i think,
would be enough.

sarai nichole

"*i no im in luv w u
bc everywhere i look
i am looking for u.
ur in evry empty chair—
wherver i am.
ur in the way the music
hurts more than it should.*

*i wud text u
but i'm afraid ur happy.
afraid u forgot
how i said ur name
like a prayer i didn't deserv.
i luv u, ok?
and i no
thats a dumb thing to say,
but if i dont say it
now youll never here it again.*

*i look for u
in evry laugh,
evry drink,
evry face i'll 4get by morning.*

*pls just
tell me u look for me to."*

i need a life that isn't just
a countdown to when it all ends.

not spent waiting for a moment
that will somehow redeem me
for all the moments i missed,
or for the ones
i didn't have the courage to seize.

i want to breathe,
to feel the rush of air,
enter my lungs
and not be taxed for it.

i want to take advantage of it all,
because what a waste it would be
to feel bad for having succeeded.

i have no interest in a retirement
that is only earned,
rarely promised.
there will never be a perfect time
to be happy.

there will never be a perfect moment
to stop asking.

i want a life where i tried,
and i lived—
not just waited.

sarai nichole

i know we'll never have the right time,
but for now, i am content
with the stolen moments,
the weight of your arms around me
while the world sleeps.

i traded the dream of morning light
for the soft hum of midnight calls,
a whispered promise in the dark,
just enough to keep me desperate.

you never asked me to stay.

and the morning always came,
but i learned how to slip away
before the sun reminded me,
that i'd never be more
than your sorry attempt to feel something.

and i knew you'd never ask
how i liked my eggs.

the museum of me

coming home from college
means stepping into a museum,
of the person you used to be.
the air feels heavier here,
saturated by the presence
of someone you're still trying to understand.

it means taking your luggage
down to the basement,
only to find your "box of things"—
letters in your twelve-year-old scrawl,
drawings with uneven lines,
and ticket stubs from movies
you barely remember watching.

it means opening the cupboard,
reaching for salt,
but finding it somewhere new.
the cookies that lived
on the bottom shelf
have finally disappeared,
but the sugar jar still clings
to the same sticky ring
it had years ago.

sarai nichole

and the kettle still clicks in the night.

in your closet,
your track and field ribbons hang limp,
faded by time,
and the fifth-grade speech award still sits on the wall,
crooked, a little smug.

on the kitchen counter,
there used to be oranges—
your mom always bought too many.
now, there's a stack of envelopes,
the kind with windows,
the kind you'll soon have to open.

but maybe later,
just for old time's sake, i'll have an orange.

excerpts from my journal

for the past year,
i've clung to a single phone call.

the one where you told me
you'd signed a contract—
something about farm maintenance,
a reason to stay rooted.
and i asked,
did that mean i could finally see you drive a tractor?

could i chase the dogs across the fields,
watch the world soften around us?

i could hear your smile through the line,
the kind that always convinced me
to hold on—
just one more day.

maybe tomorrow,
you'd spare me some gentleness.
maybe tomorrow,
you'd stop seeing the world
as something to fight against,
and let me love you without bruises.

sarai nichole

you told me
we'd have to attach a wagon
to the back of the tractor,
so i'd never be too far
from your side.

the dogs would be there too,
their tails wagging
in the dream you painted
just for me.

and i believed you.

i believed we could outrun the distance,
break the curse of the space between us—
because i knew,
as long as you gave me a reason to love you,
any reason at all,
i would follow you
to the ends of the earth.

but now,
all i have is the echo of that promise,
and the question of

why i ever thought
you'd let me stay.

excerpts from my journal

i hope you find your person.
the one who shows up enough times
that even your mind,
with all its stubborn shadows,
starts to soften,
to believe in presence over doubt.

there was a day
i sat on the edge of my bed,
panic gripping my chest,
the kind of fear
that doesn't make sense,
but takes over anyway.

and just as i thought
i might not survive it,
i thought of my best friend.

the way she never asks me
to explain the inexplicable,
how she listens without words,
how she knows when to show up
and when to stay silent.

and somehow,
the panic let go first.

sarai nichole

for the first time,
i had more control over it
than it had over me—
not because it disappeared,
but because it was outmatched
by the quiet proof
that i wasn't alone in this anymore.

because when someone shows up—
in enough moments,
in enough ways—
you realize the shadows don't have to win.

so, this is my prayer for you:
that you find someone like that.
someone who won't fix it all,
but who makes the impossible
feel just a little lighter.
i pray you find someone who stays,

and that one day,
you'll stay for yourself too.

excerpts from my journal

we do not heal without wounds.

somewhere along the way,
we began to romanticize
what we call the healing process.

i am guilty of it too,
mistaking survival for radiance.

some spill their pain into words,
others go silent—
finding pride in keeping something for themselves,
even as it festers.

some seek solace in strangers,
getting lost in eyes
that do not pry.
others place their faith
in the slow mercy of time.

yet as we name our own endurance
as something noble, something rare,
we cannot deny what made us begin—

pain.
so much pain.
a wound must open before it closes,
a body must break before it mends.

scars do not rise upon untouched skin.

sarai nichole

wait, i wasn't ready.

i only just noticed
the way the sun softens before it sets.
the way dust twirls in the late afternoon light.
the way laughter lingers in a room
even after everyone has gone.

i turned to look time in the eye,
but before i could speak,
it shoved me forward—
before i could press my palms
against the moment,
before i could tell it,
stay, just a little longer.

i wasn't done
watching the wind shake the trees.
i wasn't done
listening to the last notes of that song.

i wasn't done being here.

excerpts from my journal

you are not going
to follow me out the door.
i know that now.
but i will still leave
the knob drawn vertically.

not because i think
you'll change your mind,
but because i got used
to making it easier for you to love me.

sarai nichole

the worst part of loving
was that i didn't get the choice.

i woke up the next morning,
with a burn in my throat,
knowing this feeling wouldn't vanish
just because you did.

excerpts from my journal

in the dream i claim to forget,

you called me back.

sarai nichole

"the seats are empty.
the theatre is dark.
why do you keep acting?"

because i have perfected
this version of myself,
and i have memorized the act
for others to enjoy.
now that they have left,
i don't know how
to be anything else.

excerpts from my journal

i'm not what you need
and i'm trying
to be okay with that.

but i loved you
with all that i had,
and i'm trying to fathom
how both concepts
could be true at once.

sarai nichole

"have you ever gotten what you wanted?

no. but once, i came close."

i could've had him—
and that was the problem.
the moment he was within reach,
he lost the shape i had given him.

like a name whispered too many times,
until it sounds foreign.
like a song you swore you loved,
until you learned the lyrics.

i had to see him,
exactly as he was.
not as a promise,
not as potential,
but as a man standing before me.

and when i asked myself
if i wanted *him,*
not the version i once dreamed,
but the one who existed—

i knew.
the act of asking was already my answer.

because without the illusion,
of who he might become,
this was as close as i would ever want to be.

but what do you do with a love
that has nowhere to go?

what do you do with a heart still full
of someone you never wish to see again?

excerpts from my journal

i see her again,
head down, shoulders tight,
counting her breaths
like she's running out.

she doesn't look up.
she thinks i am another voice telling her to relax,
telling her to breathe,
telling her she worries too much
for someone so young.

i don't.

instead, i sit beside her,
fingers tracing the same wild hair
unruly as she was,
tied to the same restless mind.
i ask if she's tired.

she exhales—finally—
like she's been waiting
for someone to ask instead of stare.

i tell her nights are still long,
but we learned
to make peace with them.
and that the quiet truth is—
everyone feels just as alone.

so, when i ask her for forgiveness,
she meets me with grace.
and i tell her—
no matter what they say,
their life is not your race.

sarai nichole

i feel like a fool—
sitting here,
fists clenched,
head pounding
with the migraine-like-reminder
that i would still like to hear about your day.

did you get your usual bagel?
the bitter coffee?
*God, you hated
how i liked mine iced.*

did you roll your eyes when they asked—
"for here or to go?"

did you reach out to someone today?
or did the walls win again?

the same four walls,
the only thing
that never asked you to be better.

anyway... did you eat?

i still want to know.
God, i still want to know.

isn't that what grief is?
holding the left palm
of the stuffed bear
to your ear—

until the rasp of their voice
is crushed beneath the same weight
laid upon you?

excerpts from my journal

i figured the quiet
would be greater
than the constant noise—
the only thing we knew how to grow.

would you remind me
of all i am unworthy of being?
would you yell at me,
just once more?

slam a door of familiarity,
i beg—
or blow up my phone
during hours
i no longer cared to lose.

for your hostility,
was the only force capable enough
to stir something within me.

i no longer find comfort in quiet,
not since you.

my pulse has learned to rest
against the trusted current

of your uncertainty.

sarai nichole

cats have always intimidated me—
their effortless independence,
the quiet certainty
in the way they trust themselves without question.

they will always land
on their own four limbs, no matter the height.

i've been a dog person
for as long as i can remember.
my childhood dog
was the first to love me without condition,
and took all the blame
as she left me with a void
i mindlessly aimed to fill.

maybe that's the difference between want and need—
i wanted to know
that the things i chose to love would always be there
to love me back.

but i needed to learn how to depend
on my own devotion.

please God—
if i promise to be selfish with my heart,
will you promise me nine lives, in return?

and maybe in the next one,
they'll stay.

excerpts from my journal

there must have been progressive claims of casual—
for i do not recognize the one you possess.

you slithered your way into my behaviors,
leaving your cadence
imprinted on my tongue,
chiseled into each syllable,
your way of thinking lodged between my own.

i tore down
every mirror in sight—
no longer recognizing
the contours of my own jaw
without your fingers
tracing the outline.

and even in the comfort of my sheets,
where your body will not rest,
it's as if your scent
was threaded into each stitch of fabric
before it was ever mine.

for how long will you remain everywhere—
and nowhere?

sarai nichole

i believe the most painful loves
are the ones that end
not for the lack of love,
but for everything in between.

you want to be angry—
for the job they accepted,
for the country they moved to,
for choosing their mother's side over yours,
for admitting they can't love you
the way you deserve,
for being allergic to the dogs
you refuse to live without.

but that's exactly why you love them,
and that's exactly why it hurts.
because of the unspoken knowing—

that our love alone,
will not be the thing that saves us.

excerpts from my journal

but what if i've done it all wrong?
poured myself into hands unsteady,
fueled the wrong fires,
and chased dead ends
thinking they'd be ready?

how do we know for sure
that we're on the right track—
navigating a maze
whose exit is a metaphor,
whose strangers are riddles
we were never meant to solve?

what if i crave the vices that kill?
what if i wake with a heart too heavy
to bear the weight of will?

what if i give him ten chances
and the next one—none?
what if kindness is finite
and i no longer have a ton?

how do we know when it's too late?
do we prolong this death,
or fall victim,
to what we've claimed to be fate?

sarai nichole

i think family
is more than just the ones
we're born to love—
as honest as genetics can be.

and i think love
is about the ones you forgive,
and forgive again.
not because you accept all their wrongs,
but because the good
has outweighed the bad
every time.

and for as honest
as you would take them—
knowing they could never give you
more than what they were—
your greatest act of love
was always to outweigh.

i have loved you
more than your wrongs.
more than your wretched excuses.
more than your harsh words,
on even harsher days.

even when i
pull my shoulder away
as you try to shed your guilt,
i will still wish you goodnight.

excerpts from my journal

to see so much of yourself in someone else—
not by blood,
but by bond—
to feel tied to them
in ways the body cannot prove,
and still believe in them
the way they once believed in you.

it was never about apologies,
for it would be cruel
to ask someone
for what you know they did not possess.

no—
this was devotion.

maybe not in its purest form,
but surely in its most transparent of skins.

my biggest act of love was seeing you naked—
not beyond the eyes of intimacy,
but beyond pretense—
flaws bared, flesh worn,
and, still
loving you for worse.

sarai nichole

i wish i had the chance to meet my father,
when his innocence
was still able to protect me
from rage that had yet to be woken.

and in another life, i did.

i walked through streets
where dirt and anger built the houses ahead.
where breath was held,
instead of taken.
and in my search for peace,
i found him first.

a little boy, licking the salt
from his own tears—
as if they always outran him.
his two left feet,
balancing on the beam
above shallow waters.

i reached for him.

"get down," i whispered.
and for a singular moment in time,
i saw myself in him.

a permanent frown, a busted lip,
a scarred chin,
an eyebrow still split.

"you are beautiful," i told him.
"you are so brave."
"and you are gentle, no matter how tough
you feel you ought to be."

he wrapped his arms around me.
he offered me his pinky.
"it won't last forever," i promised.

he pulled away—
"my dad once told me the same thing."

i wanted so badly to say,
"then be the thing that saves you."

but instead, i rose.
i left him there,
with words too soft to stop the storm.
i gave him forgiveness,
in advance.

unluckily,
it did not reach
the life i was born to live.

sarai nichole

one day, it'll all make sense.

anxiety will still sit in the corner—
occasionally mistaking panic for preparation,

it will come,
but it will also go.

most of the people you love now
will not be there in a few years.
this one will sting—
but in time,
you'll come to understand that not everyone
is meant to stay.

some people are only passing through,
leaving fingerprints on the doorframe,
but never stepping inside.

remember,
you cannot predict people's reactions
to your boundaries,
but you can control your own.

and mom—
mom, who has always been there,
who warned you about all the things
you swore would never touch you,
who told you that one day,
you'd thank her for the hardships.

excerpts from my journal

and one day, you do.

you will love,
and be loved.
but once again,
it will be learnt—
sometimes
you'll have to disappoint the people you love,
in order to love yourself.

but do not fear,
for this is not failure.
rather,
it is the most brave
act of adoration one can bear.

and if loss is inevitable,
then let it find you full.

with love, you—

just older, softer, and waiting.

sarai nichole

echolalia of love

you do not have to shed your skin
for others to grasp the time they've lost.
you do not have to push the earth forward,
only aid built out of your own will.

God did not leave Adam unaccompanied.
he does not ask you to give
what was never pressed,
into the hollow of your palm.

what is love,
if not the echolalia
of our greatest companions?

what is love,
if not the bullets
we do not question,
for those we meet again after death?

excerpts from my journal

what is love,
if not my life, for yours?

i will welcome golden gates
before i am expected,
to live in a world
you were not built to withstand.

perhaps love is euphoria.
but i am no drug addict.

perhaps when life feels like it's ending,

it has simply been too long
since you last rested your head,
in the lap of your dearest friend.

sarai nichole

sometimes,
i like to think
that maybe, just maybe—
you let me go
because you knew i would never reach for better.

i would've loved you exactly as you were,
for as long as you'd let me.

and had i stayed, ultimately,
that would've ended in death.

i no longer stood
behind rose-colored glasses,
no white picket fence between you and i.
no reflection in shining armor.
you did not fight.

why didn't you fight?

and God, the love i built for you—
never pure,
but always consuming,
always earnest.

i wanted to love you.
and you wanted me dead.

and now, i fear
i would have died in honor,
for i was always
a trying woman.

i suppose i should thank you for
putting me out of a misery
i was not ready to meet.

i no longer love you.
and that should frighten you much more.

sarai nichole

you will not write me love letters, no matter
how many times i remind you

i am a poet.

you do not wish of me.
not in a way i recognize.
not in any way that feeds me,
only in a way that does not starve.

you do not speak my language,
no matter how many translations i offer,
each one ignored,
each one unread.
and you brace my hands like artifacts—
like something to own,
never to uncover.

and still,
i would remain,
for as long as you would invite me.
like a book you will not read,
but will not let anyone else hold.

you will not extend kindness
to each knuckle in offering—
for you do not believe in tenderness,
where there is no transaction.

and you will not lower your voice,
*yet perish the thought
i ever curse you in return.*

you will always flinch at the sound of love
when it is not on your terms.
when it is not woken
during the hours
belonging only to the moon.

and God forbid
i cross the line you drew in sand,
and call it permanence.

as you are not gentle, only ever a man.

and i
am no longer waiting for love
to be pried from clenched fists.

you will not write me love letters.
you never could.

*so let me leave, before i forget
what it feels like to be wanted.*

sarai nichole

what a privilege it is
to learn from those
who have known suffering
so that i would not.

those who spare us
wounds and marked flesh,
who take the blade
before it ever reaches our skin.

how many times have i spoke freely,
because someone before me
swallowed more than just their words?

how many nights have i slept soundly,
because another spent a life
that did not know rest?

and still,
i complain of hunger,
while my plate is plenty full.

i still wince at the weight of survival,
though i was never the one who carried it.

*"maybe i am just a woman,
but i would really like to be angry.
God, i would like to be angry."*

but i needed to be more.
"angry" would not suffice.

i wanted to curse, to bare teeth.
i wanted to throw in the towel,
and i wanted to be *praised for it.*

all without apology,
all with the same love i am given now.

isn't it ironic,
the way we've begged the man
to state the feminine?

would my anger be as criminal
as my alleged need for defiance?
or is defiance only rebellion
when it's a woman who refuses to kneel?

sarai nichole

i do not yearn for violence,
i yearn for a voice
that does not remain missed
by even those who do not speak.

perhaps all this anger was once love.
perhaps i did not need violence
as much as it needed me.

but if it is anger that will validate me,
then forgive the smirk
that itches the corners of my lips
when you find yourself displeased.

for i have lived a lifetime
in your *momentary displeasure.*

you do not get to call me disturbed,
when you've always preferred me insane.

excerpts from my journal

if i can't be the thing that saves you,
let me offer you comfort before you go.

i pour the cream into your coffee
with trembling hands
and a shake to my breath.
and i pretend
you don't hear me sniffling from the kitchen.

i look to you,
as if each moment may be our last,
because we both know how this will end.

i tell you that i forgive you
because i know you need to hear it,

but i pray to Gods
i'm not sure you believe in,

just in case
someone's still listening.

sarai nichole

i would run after you in a burning building,
and i would sacrifice myself,
need be.

but this isn't fire.
it's water.
and you've been drowning for years.

and i've never been a strong swimmer.

so i sit on the shore,
watching the waves pull you under,
wondering if the ache in my chest
is grief
or guilt
or both.

because love can't be a life raft
if someone's already let go.

excerpts from my journal

i ask myself
if i am capable of being a mother—
not just a mom.

but the woman of perfectionism,
asks me if i can be calm—
if i can focus on all things at once,
if i can prioritize myself
over someone who will always need me more.

i pause.

"what if it stops with me?"

i look around the room.

the plants in the window
stretch towards the light,
thriving in soil i turned,
in water i remembered to give.
they bloom
because i wanted them to.

i pass my sister's door,
her walls cluttered with the growing pains
of a girl still deciding
who she wants to be.

but in the way she laughs when i do—

sarai nichole

she chose me
as someone worth becoming.

and then—
i think about my mother.
not in some glowing,
untouchable light.

but as a woman
who loved me loud enough
to drown out the quieter pain,
she never let me see.
and maybe
that's all the proof i need.

because love, the right kind,
never leaves bruises— it builds.

it ends with me.
not because it must,
but because it already did.

excerpts from my journal

february 17, 2025.

laying in the space belonging to my little sister
on days where her absence lingers,
i feel fifteen again.

the colors here hum,
loud against the cracked posters
and tangled string lights.
the walls almost breathe,
alive in a way mine never were.

and i wonder
when i became so hollow.

my walls are elegant, neutral, measured—

like they're performing peace instead of living it.

sarai nichole

but hers—
hers are raw.

layers of impulsive color,
sunlight spilling in recklessly,
like the room doesn't know
it'll go dark later.

as i lay here,
between sprawled sheets and sunken pillows,
the scent of coconut and big dreams still lingering,
i feel time stretching out again.

and for a moment,
i'm not rushing.
i'm not hollow.

i just—
have time.

poetry unveils me
only as much as i will allow.

my pen does not stop writing
despite the weight of words.
it does not falter,
or ask for a moment to breathe.

artistry is often a cry for help
overpowered by applause.
some call it beautiful,
clapping with damp palms,
but always leaving
just before the lights go back on.

look but don't touch.
don't ever get too close.

my words give me distance.
they let me carve pain
into something palatable—
no collar, no tag,
no clear address.

so you may never know if this ache is mine,
or if i'm simply the messenger.

sarai nichole

but you'll feel it.
and that's the point.

to give name to your suffrage
even if not from your lips.
to let yourself burn,
from the ashes of a fire
you did not set.

because if you break here,
if your ribs crack open
under the weight of a stranger's words,
you won't have yourself to blame.

because if it hurts here,
you don't have to ask why.

if i can share the pain i did not ask for,

maybe you can too.

excerpts from my journal

i cannot invite you to my wedding,
because it is supposed to be
the happiest day of my life.

"when two hearts become one,"
or however the saying goes.

from as early as i can remember,
i wanted to be a bride.

not for the applause nor the attention,
but for the belief that i too,
could promise myself to more than a man
who could not keep his word—
let alone a vow.

and i still believe—
one day,
when the time is right,
i'll be ready.

but you will not be there.

how could i possibly
give my heart to another,
knowing the invisible string
is still tethered to the stranger
sitting in the furthest corner?

sarai nichole

how can i vow to love,
to cherish,
to *trust*—
when you once promised me the same,
and now you do not stand before me?

even if you stay silent,
even if you bow your head
when the priest offers objections,

i will hear you.
louder than the vows,
louder than the applause.

and as the tears soak through my veil—
the ones my husband will believe
are for him—
you and i will know.

and that is a line i will not cross.

i cannot invite you to my wedding,
because i am no longer your bride—

but a part of me will always grieve that i almost was.

excerpts from my journal

i do not know how to write
when i am anything
but shattered.

when my mind forces me
to spare some of its weight onto paper.
and maybe it's because grief sells,
and sorrow lingers?

perhaps the weight of the world
falls upon one too many shoulders,
whereas internal happiness
likes to be chased—
never caught.

when i'm happy,
i do not wish to be confined.
i don't feel the need to hide her away.
she prefers when i do not acknowledge,

just be.

sarai nichole

but agony—
she is never far behind.
silently stepping along each footprint in the sand
until my legs grow tired.

until i am forced to selfishly invite others
into the darkness,
dressed as the sun.

there is no light
at the end of this tunnel—
but together, there is warmth.

i haven't figured out how to write about what does not follow,
and the sun prefers to be the hunted.

excerpts from my journal

i promise not to blame you for staying,
if you promise to confide.

i will not call him a monster—
even under rose-colored glasses,
your pain could never be shielded.

i will not call you cowardly.
it takes more courage
than most will ever know
to love someone for better,
and for the worst.

i will not call you cowardly—
because i have had to be brave before:
painting different pictures
when asked different questions,
remembering to tread lightly
just in case i had to return.

sarai nichole

when they call you weak,
i will call you strong.

how selfless, how brave,
how deeply empathetic you must be—
to endure bruises and unkind words
and still believe in the very hands laid upon you.

so i will not judge.
i will sit beside you in the silence,
in the storm,
in the healing.

i will pray with you.
i will pray for you.
and i will pray
for those who come after you.

excerpts from my journal

when i consider that you are the only person
i have not yet found it in me
to forgive,
i wonder if others have ever struggled
to extend the same hand, my way.

i question if i have left wounds naked to the eye,
damage that no apology
could ever mend,
simply because
my skin laid mangled first?

i remind myself
that some of the best people i have known,
have hurt others,
during their greatest attempt at love.

i imagine those i've hurt,
praying to something bigger than them,
not to save me,
but to free themselves of me.
and then i wonder if it freed them,
in a way i could never be.

maybe i should learn to offer grace.
but you never taught me how—
only how to ask for it.

they tell me all this anger will only hurt me,
that i will never find peace like this—

sarai nichole

as if i don't already know what it has cost me.

can't you see me trying?

if only the tire they pointed out
beneath my eyes
could reach them.

i have been angry
for as long as i can remember.
i have settled for my own form of peace.

nostalgia has become
the bane of my existence,
yet i cannot filter through.
i am made up
of every brilliant and terrible thing
that has ever happened to me.

i wish it was merely an identity crisis
that excused all this rage,
but it always comes down to a fear
i cannot ignore.

if i am to shed this anger,
if i offer the same forgiveness
i all but begged for in dormant,

who will be angry for the little girl, that lives within me?

excerpts from my journal

he wasn't a bad person,
he just wasn't *her* person,
and she hated knowing that.

because he was respectful
and always kind,
always reassuring,

and always emotionally blind.

she needed fire,
someone who could handle her
when she became too much for herself.

somebody who could offer her
more than love,
something other than a dream.
someone who could meet her,
because they'd met themselves even deeper.

he wasn't a bad person
and his love was never questioned,
yet she couldn't help but wonder—

was she truly meant for him,
or to bound be another lesson?

sarai nichole

someone always has to love the other person more.
and this time, it's me.

because the first time, it was you,
and apparently that wasn't enough.

to familiarize myself
with the danger i always craved,
i went running full speed ahead
until you could not decipher,
my breath,
for the smoke.

i did not come out
until i was charred to the core.
until i had burnt any remnants
of skin i could never shed.

excerpts from my journal

you were there waiting for me,
just liked i knew you'd be.
but you were cold as ice,
a form i did not recognize.

you feared my need for chase.
feared that the cold
which now surrounded you,
could never hold me close.

that i would always ache to be burned.

i didn't know how to tell you
that i was overheating,
that my body
was now longing for the cold.

because when you
stood at the perfect temperature,
i could not settle for comfort.

how foolish of me.

sarai nichole

the art of distraction

i pull my hair as tightly as it will go,
until i decide it's good enough
and head for the door.
i do not check my phone.

tonight, i will try to live.

my friends have poured me a drink,
i finish it before they can pour theirs
and i do not check my phone.

i am desperate for their laughter,
making a fool of myself
in hopes that the smile they bear
will reach deep within me,
and that it will be enough to busy my mind.

we bump shoulders
hauling our drunken selves into a taxi
one seat too short.
but no one moves,
no one says anything.

the same way no one questions
when i check my phone
just for the time,
but they know better.

we dance the night away.

excerpts from my journal

laughing with strangers,
making friends in bathrooms with girls
who tell me i'm beautiful—
and i thank them
before returning the favor.

there is an itch in my palm,
but i do not check my phone.

i will not sleep alone tonight,
one of my girlfriends has invited me to stay over.
and though i thank her audibly,
i thank her again, inwardly,
again and again,
until my eyes lay to rest.

it is not until
i feel her soft,
even breaths, beside me,
that i reach out.

heading straight for the search bar—
"beautiful"
i look for in our messages,
the ones from way back when.

i allow myself to fall asleep
phone in hand,
dreaming of a time
when i still believed in the power of words.

sarai nichole

my therapist told me that it's okay to cry.

i told her i know this already,
but i won't—

i cannot let them win.

she asks me whom i speak of,
who could possibly win a battle
they did not know was started?

but you would know.
you always knew.

i laugh, audibly,
and she picks up that damn pen,
once again.

she must think i'm crazy.
she'll probably try to up my meds,
and i will comply,
hoping it'll settle the ache that lies within her—
the one she's holding out for me.

excerpts from my journal

it won't do much of course,
i have been numb for far too long.

i envy the hope in her eyes—
the silent prayer
that maybe this time,

she will outsmart me.

maybe the next session,
i will say what she's waiting to hear.
maybe i will let her believe
that she is changing me
in ways no one else ever has.

maybe i will give her the kind of hope
that was once meant for me.

and as i watch her fall apart just the same,
i almost want to ask her how it feels.

sarai nichole

when he would get angry—
with me,
with the world, with those
who were just trying to love him,
it was always:

"you don't even know me."

but i was no fool.
he could not handle being seen under a light
he could not adjust to his liking.

one that could not hide
the distortions of his true being.

the one that was *scared,*
the man who forced his demons
upon those around him,
in hopes they would choose
a different lamb for sacrifice.

he longed for company
that would devote themselves to his inner work.

so if they failed,
it would be their loss and still his gain.

excerpts from my journal

unluckily for us both,
i would only ever grow to become
the thing he's truly afraid of.

i was never a fixer.
never someone who mistook his ruin
for something waiting to be rebuilt.

and that threatened the man.

because if i was right about him,
then he would have to be wrong.
if i was real,
then his lies would bear no weight.

and so,
he could never love me.
because loving me
would have meant facing himself.

and that was the one thing we both knew,
would bring him to his knees.

the act of submission to their raw being,
would always be the greatest threat,

to the man.

sarai nichole

the trauma bond

never an explanation
just an excuse.
to endure, to sacrifice,
to accept—
knowingly.

you were not the first to see my scars
and love me anyways.

but you were the only one who made space for
the girl still hiding inside me.
and i could not help
but see you as the boy
who was given all the wrong lessons on love.

we were not trying to love each other.
we were trying to save each other.

and maybe that's why we held on for so long.
because no one else could understand why we stayed.
why we mistook survival
as a purpose destined for us both.

excerpts from my journal

to them, it was toxic.
to us, it was the only language we both knew.

while others saw only what we had become,
we knew trauma
was never just about what happened—

it was about what never left.

what lingered in the way we spoke,
the way we flinched,
the way we loved
with our hands half-closed.

staying felt like a responsibility,
but it was never ours to own.

it was not my burden,
but i refused to fail the boy
who saw the girl in me
as something still worth holding.

so when he wrapped his arms around me
in his own attempt at closure,

i let him,
and i did not flinch.

if staying for me
would teach him the ultimate act of love,
then i would remain still,
for as long as he would stand with me.

sarai nichole

and when the time comes
where i have learned
all i was meant to know,

as my last wish—
dress me in my wedding gown.
if i have yet to be married,
mermaid style will do,
let my best friend pick it out.

and please,
do not forget to place
my graduation cap on my head
in a way that does not conceal my curls.

make sure that i am holding
a dog's leash in one hand,
maybe a ball to throw,
in the other.

as i have many walks to make up for,
and many milestones to be seen
by those who occupied all my empty seats.

excerpts from my journal

*"when you die,
who will sit at your grave the longest?"*

i would like to say my mother,
but i am not her only child.
and though she would wear her grief
like a badge of honor,
for longer than i'd ever have wanted,

a mother—
she would always have to be.

perhaps it would be
the friends i have known the longest,
but i know they would lower my casket
and tread back to their homes
with heavy feet,
where they could grieve in silence.
*the awkwardness that accompanied vulnerability—
one of the many things we would always share.*

my lover would remain
long after the service had ended.
yet eventually, in honor of my wishes,
he would gather his heart,
piece by piece,
from the ruins around me,
and find comfort in what distance
could never replace.

and still, every anniversary,
his beautiful wife,
holding their children that inherited his rosy cheeks
and soft ways—
the ones we had already named—
would eat sandwiches on the grass
and tell me stories.

sarai nichole

but my best friend—
dressed in the darkest,
most beautifully haunting shades of blacks,
she would stand still.

she'd look up to the heavens,
grey clouds blocking her line of sight,
tears brimming those big blue eyes,
begging and pleading,

and ask God why.

she would go over every conversation,
read through every message
until the words blurred into nothing.
she would listen to old voicemails,
just to hear me breathe,
perhaps to spot a tremble—
and play back our last conversation,
pausing, rewinding,
trying to find the moment i slipped away.

she would sit in her childhood room,
tearing pages from her journal,
the same ones i once told her
would make people feel less alone.

yet alone, she now sat.

enveloped in her mother's trying arms,
the only thing keeping her here,
but never enough to save her.

and even if she chose to live on, for me,
despite me,

it would never again be *with* me.
it would never again be enough.

*"when i read
that we need salt
and water to live,
i thought,
how poetic of God
to put them both in our tears."*

i read this repeatedly,
until i thought maybe
i could look past the irony.

maybe if i read over the lines
until they all blurred together,
the beauty this writer describes
would show itself to me.

and yet,
i have stared at this poem for days,
and still i cannot fathom—

the irony of relying
on salt and water for survival,
the secret being the tears we let fall.

because i have cried great rivers,
and fear that i have not lived a day.

sarai nichole

there's a gentleness,
to the act of naming a child
after something that you found solace in.

in an odd, but simple sense—
we essentially love something,
or someone,
so much,
that we remember them in
what we believe will be ours forever.
even if *they* can't be.

how special one must be—
to be named after something
someone planned to be
their greatest act of love.

excerpts from my journal

i just need to know—
when did you wake up
and realize that i loved you?

you'll never say it, at least not to me.
and i have learned to live with that,
so please don't find your voice now.

because there was a time
when i would have done anything to hear it.
when i would have let those words
undo me completely.

but i have moved on.
i am happy. i am okay.
i am loved, loudly.
and i deserve to be.

there is a part of me that will always wonder—
if you had loved me then,
if you had been who i needed then,
would i have ever needed anyone else?

but i do not live in that place anymore.
and i cannot go back.
not even for you.

sarai nichole

you will always know
that you were my greatest weakness.
and i think you are starting to realize
that a part of me will always be yours, too.

i guess the only question left, is,
when did you wake up
and realize that *you* loved *me?*

do not make me remember
who i used to be for you.
do not make me wonder
what could have been—

when i have already learned
how to live with what is.

so if you must speak—
do not speak to me.

perspective.
the one thing that always challenged me.

to know, or not to know?

i was never good
at admitting my wrongs,
and i mean *really feeling them*—
not just voicing them.

at least not until i was the one,
asking another
to bear their sins to me,
as though singing a prayer.

and an offer of perspective
often made people
do just that.

i just needed to hear it—
to know that it was real,
to know that my feelings were valid,
to hurt enough
to never look back.

but the distant memory,
still makes my insides cave.

sarai nichole

and yet—
sometimes,
i still wanted to know
if you thought of me.

if you had ever called her by name
while swearing
"it was only a mistake."

do you ever dream
of a world where i still remained?

do you apologize
in that one?

if i dream of you,
does it really mean
you still think of me?

do you ever get flash backs
to *that* night?

do you still remember your promises,
and did you promise her the same?
was she too,
slowly beating you at your own game?

or was it all
just my perspective?

excerpts from my journal

the sun woke up
around the same time i did today.

i only knew this
because i could feel the warm air
reflecting off my window,
dancing with the shadows of the sun.

and i swear i heard a bird chirp.

three days
in the solace of my bed—
in great company, nevertheless,
with my dog
and the impending doom of writer's block.

i will go outside,
perhaps.
maybe if sit on my front porch
and put my headphones on,
focusing on only the warmth
splayed across my face,

mentally,
i will not be where my feet lay planted.

sarai nichole

maybe i'll go buy a new plant.
i've been really into ivies lately.

maybe i'll discover a coffee shop
that smells like the pages of an old book,
and sit in a chair that wobbles,
until i catch myself

enjoying the moment,
without wondering if anyone sees me.

maybe today,
i will ask my mother
if she'd like company running errands,
and i will leave my hair
out of its usual too-tight of a bun,
and offer it to the wind, instead.

i did not close my blinds tonight,
and the sun was still out, at six pm.

maybe everything will be okay.
and i look forward to tomorrow.

excerpts from my journal

hate can be forgotten,
but imprints are the work of love.

and it's true,
any love i gave you was always yours to keep.
and God knows,
i gave you all of it.

i let you carve your name into my future,
tie strings around my wrists,
and pull me tighter each time i thought to leave.

i would have given you everything—
and i did.
my softness, my certainty,
the girl i was before you.

i would have burned myself down,
just to be warm enough for you
to find me inviting, again.

but you could never be just mine.

you craved the idea of love,
but never the reality of it.
and i refused to look closely enough to see the difference.

still, i can't find it in me
to wish it had gone any differently.

because truth be told—
you saved me.

sarai nichole

not in the way i wanted,
but in the way i needed.

you saved me from wasting more years
chasing the love
you would only ever dangle in front of me.

you saved me from falling
into the same pattern,
from spending my life
thinking that love was something i had to earn.

you showed me what love could be—
and what love should never become.
you taught me my worth,
by failing to see it.

and in every part of me you could not love,
i have learned to love myself,
that much more.

so keep it.
every ounce of love i ever gave you.
i do not need it back.

and perhaps one day,
this will save another one
of your hopelessly romantic victims.

or maybe, we both will.

but i will reach for them
while they can still return.
and you will only ever show them
how to live with the damage.

excerpts from my journal

but i can't love you, anymore.

because i have spent
most of the time—
since i have truly been alive,
feeling you build your nest
in my subconscious.

and every part of me that wants you
knows that a time not long ago,
she could not have you.

so,
i will not watch these tables turn,
because i am no longer seated
where you left me.

sarai nichole

my cousins and i
have made an unspoken commitment
to seeing one another,
whenever we have the chance,
now that we're old enough.

and every moment
i spend with them,
heals something within me.

this time around,
i made sure to bring my camera.
they all laughed and sighed the same,
when i told them to pose,

but their smiles couldn't be missed.
no longer crooked, still forced,
yet somehow even brighter.

when we were younger,
all the things that went on
behind closed doors,
tended to keep us from one another's.

excerpts from my journal

if only they could see us now.

together, by choice,
making up for every year we spent too far apart.

learning each other's quirks again,
piecing together old stories,
realizing how much time we missed—
and through shared losses—

how much that time mattered.

so, we stay longer, we hug tighter,
and we leave slower.

never because we have to,
always because we want to.

and maybe, if nothing else,
this is proof
that we were always meant to find our way back home—

now that we're old enough.

sarai nichole

is it selfish—
to truly wish for them to move on
but still hope that they don't forget you?

and i mean it.
i want them to move on.
i do.

but it's been two years now,
and a part of me still aches to be remembered fondly—
not mourned, not regretted,
just not erased.

i gave so much of myself,
and when it ended,
i had learn how to close the door alone.
no final words.

and that's fine.
that's life.
some people leave,
and some people forget.

but still—
i hope i cross his mind
in the quiet moments.
not often, not painfully,
just enough—
i still exist somewhere,
a distant voice,
a feeling he can't place.

i hope i was more than something to leave behind.

i hope i was something worth remembering.

excerpts from my journal

we were almost something,
almost right,
almost enough to make it work.

and maybe that's why it hurts more—
because the almosts
never give you answers,
never give you closure.

when love ends, you at least know why.

but almosts—
they leave you stranded in the what ifs;
in the stories you tell yourself
just to make sense of the silence.

there was no big fight,
no moment where it all fell apart.
just a slow fade,

a hesitation that lasted too long,
until one day, it was just over—
or maybe it never really began.

sarai nichole

i don't know if we could have worked,
but i hate that i'll never know.
that's the part that lingers—
not love,
not hope,
just the not knowing.

so now, at night,
i rewrite our ending in my head,
trying to figure out which version hurts the least.

which one lets me sleep.

but in the morning,
it always ends the same way—
me staring at a screen
that never lights up with your name,

still trying to wake up from a dream
that was never ours to begin with.

excerpts from my journal

you ask me for just—
one more.

and i laugh—
i could never get enough of you.

but i say no,
proud of the woman standing before me,
no longer the girl kneeling for a man
who would never even think
of lowering his pride,
just enough to meet her gaze.

you ask me just—
once more.

you told me
it would stay between just us.

sarai nichole

but that was exactly
what was wrong here.
we tended to let one too many things
stay between *just us.*

yet it never seemed
like you suffered
as much as i always did.

but i am awake now,
and though my years have been few,

i have lived a thousand lives—
and in everyone,
i have watched you leave.

once more would never be enough.
not for you,
and certainly, not for me.

at first, i was his masterpiece.
running his hands over my ruin,
tracing the fractures
like they were deliberate,
like the damage was something to be admired.

he said he had never seen himself so clearly
until he looked at me.
i was his guilted excuse
for witnessing destruction up close
without facing his own.
a way to call something broken—
beautiful—
so he would not have to stand cursed alone.

and for a while,
i let him.
let him stand before me,
parading my so-called beauty,
before whoever would validate his gaze.

mistaking the way he lingered for love,
when all he wanted was proof.
proof that someone could be shattered
and still belong in the hands of another.

but men like him don't bear weight,
unless they built the wreckage.

sarai nichole

all those years of repressing
requires too much space,
for the burden of another's work.

and when he realized my cracks were too deep,
my canvas too layered with the hands
that came before him,
he grew restless.

so he found *her*:
a canvas patiently waiting for his signature.
something he could claim,
something that would hold only
his colors,
his mistakes,

his ravage.

and i remained—
a masterpiece only in hindsight,
a work too complete to be repainted,
too unwilling to be remade.

because the only beauty
he'd ever crave
was in the whites of welcomed reflection,

and i was never meant to be a mirror.

excerpts from my journal

i fear i will always be remembered
as the bad influence friend.

not the hand that pulled you from the edge,
but the one that led you closer.

i thought i was giving you an out,
a way to escape the weight you never spoke of.
i never asked,
and you never told me.
was that your fault, or mine?

i would've sworn i was saving you—
that pulling you from your four-walled sorrow
was a kindness,
that noise was better than silence,
that movement meant survival.

but maybe that was my method of escapism,
and not your drink of choice.

did i bring you back to life,
or teach you how to run from it?

sarai nichole

i told myself that i was helping—
that pulling you from the quiet was mercy,
that a distraction was as good as a cure.

i never meant
to be the weight on your shoulders,
the whisper in your ear,
the excuse in your mouth.

i didn't see it then.
i was too busy getting lost in your smile,
to notice the way your eyes slowly dulled.

they say it was *"never that serious."*
just a joke,
just a name,
just a thing we say.

but i can't help but wonder—
when the fun is over,
when the paths have all been chosen—
if you'll look back
and see me as the reason yours was lost.

was it my fault for never asking,
or yours for never saying no?

excerpts from my journal

the other day,
i was scrolling past something
that instantly reminded me of you,
and it stopped me cold.

in times that feel like decades ago,
where your love didn't feel like
a spoken curse each time it left my mouth,
i would've sent it to you—
awaiting your opening, your laugh,
that made my eyes smile at the sound.

but i can't do that anymore.

and still,
it felt wrong to not acknowledge it at all.

maybe it was true,
that forgiveness for yourself
did not mean erasure in totality—

it meant embracing moments like this,
only for a moment,
before scrolling past,
and letting something new spark your interest.

love and light, and let it go.

sarai nichole

you're not crazy, darling.

*you're just trying to find a place
for all those big emotions;
somewhere beyond,
or perhaps between,
your heart and your mind.*

*you aren't lost,
you're just trying to feel as alive
as you once did in your teenage years
but in a new body—
one you haven't grown into just yet.*

*still, you have time.
you have so much time.*

*and even if you don't,
live as if you do.*

excerpts from my journal

i look up, and i laugh
because i know you're laughing too,
at me, for crying so much
when you're *finally okay,*

but i worry
that you can hear each thought
as it comes, unfiltered—
and that you know too much.

that you know a part of me died
around the same time you did—

and i don't know how to live without her.

but you're alive
in all my favorite people,
and that almost brings me
the same comfort as your hold.

almost.

maybe just this once,
almost can be enough.

sarai nichole

grief is cruel in the way it rewrites memory.

how it turns love into a lie,
how it forces you to look back
on every moment
and wonder if you were the only one
who didn't know the truth.

i thought i was the only one who knew him like that.
i thought i was the only one he wanted to know.
i believed love was something you could hold onto,
as long as you held it tight enough.

i thought love made me different,
that i was his only exception—

but that's the thing
about always trusting yourself
to love honestly—
you expect others to do the same.

until you find out they never had to.

we did not love the same person.
we did not fight for the same love.
we did not mourn the same man.
we loved the pieces of him that fit us best.

i loved the one who was afraid to lose me.
she loved the one who never feared leaving.
another loved the one who swore he had changed.
another *still* loved the one who swore he never would.

but a man who is everything,
is just a man who is nothing at all.

sarai nichole

i've come to believe that some people
are meant to find you.
even in the worst ways,
especially then.

no one else will ever understand
the language of this grief.
the way it makes you question
your own name,
your own memories,
your own worth.

but they did.
they knew before i ever had to say it,
because they had been here before,
long before me.
because we had all once been in this mess together,
without even knowing.

maybe the story was never meant to end with him.
the cruelest thing he did was lie.
the kindest thing he did was lead me to them.

because in the process of trying to save myself,
i saved them too.
and without even meaning to, they pulled me from a ruin
that was much too familiar to them.

this is what he left me with:
a heart that did not have to break alone.

the greatest gift
he never meant to give me.

excerpts from my journal

"i do not hold grudges.

*you did not affect me enough
for me to learn how to hate you.*

i forgive you."

but the truth is,
i did.

i let the anger settle inside me
until i couldn't tell where it ended
and i began.
i withheld so much forgiveness,
because it was easier to hate myself, instead.

the anger outlived the apology,
and still,
i kept feeding it.

i thought my anger was holding them accountable.
i thought holding onto the pain kept me in control,
but it only ever kept me buried beneath it.

i couldn't see it at the time,
but i was the only one still suffering.

oftentimes, it is easier to blame others
than to admit that you played a part—
even if all that was left of your role
was the damage.

sarai nichole

so now,
i owe no one an explanation for my forgiveness.

because when i was suffering alone,
they told me this was what *peace* felt like.

but i have learned—
some do not want you to heal.

they need you to stay angry,
to keep the grudge breathing,
to keep the story alive.
because they do not know who they are
without their anger.

but my peace was never meant
to be a sacrifice at their altar of resentment.

i do not belong there anymore.

and if my healing makes them uncomfortable,
they were never on my side to begin with,
but that is no longer my concern.

i will not hate any longer,
because even if they deserved it,
i did not.

this is not an act of mercy.
this is me choosing to live.

love that waits

sometimes, when we're on the phone
and it's late at night—
when i am sung to sleep
by your soft snoring,
still much too loud—
i let myself fall asleep,
and dream of when we were seventeen again.

before the hour-long commutes,
and one too many red lights—

before the future we dreamed of
was just inches beyond reach,
before life stopped living in the rearview.

when our only competition
was the fellow prom king and queen go-getters,
and not our very selves.

i am *so* proud of the man snoring before me,
exhausted from blessings and accomplishments,

but sometimes i miss the boy
who stayed up all night
tangling me up into his arms
and yearning for belly laughs.

and some nights, i miss the girl
who hadn't yet let herself fall
into the calloused hands of others.

sarai nichole

who chose the boy
that ensured his mom kept all her favorite snacks
in their home,
allergies accounted for—
the first time.

whose door code she still knew.

instead of the boys
who only saw her value with the lights off.

and though we found forgiveness in adulthood,
even though
the high-school sweethearts
came home to one another
in *our* version,

sometimes,
when i go to sleep,
beside the only man
who has ever loved me properly,

i still search for the innocence we once knew.

excerpts from my journal

some parents were never meant to have children.

but she was born anyway,
and she was never just a daughter.

her hands, too small to hold the weight,
still carried it.
her future, too big for four walls,
still shrank itself down to fit.

she spoke of life
as though it ended at the parent's front door.

as if the horizon was a thing
only the *lucky ones* got to chase.

as if she was meant to stay
because *someone* had to.

but i told her—
one day, you will leave.
and you will see how small this town really was.

you will see that your toughest battles
were not chains,
but blueprints.

that being the one who stays,
the one who loves,
the one who never runs—

it did not make you weak.
it made you a safe place.

sarai nichole

it made you someone
the world will be lucky to know.

and now,
she has built her very existence
with her own hands.
she has crafted a life beyond the one
they tried to give her.

and she hasn't even realized it yet.

but i see it—
the way the world is running towards her,
the way the sky no longer looks so grey.

so i tell her,
go.

go as far as you need to.
go until you no longer feel like you are running.
go until you are simply moving forward.

and though i will miss her *dearly,*
i would never forgive her if she stayed.

so get ready for her world.
and please be kind.

excerpts from my journal

make sure you find a partner
that sits with you,
when you cannot stand by yourself.

the other night,
i found myself spiraling
into the all-too-familiar feeling of grief.
tear after tear fell quicker
than i could blink them away.

i watched as he stood at the edge of my grief,
hands open, ready to catch what he could—
but unprepared for its weight.

he didn't know what to say.
he only knew that leaving
was never an option.

some grief cannot be spoken.
some aches cannot be reasoned with.
they can only be met.

sarai nichole

he went on to tell me—
it was okay to cry,
to feel things as heavily as i did,
because my grief was a reminder
of the love that once was.

a love that could never be forgotten.
a forever keepsake, *just for me.*

he simply met me where i was,
and reminded me of what i failed to consider.

some people go, and some people stay.
and i have never been alone in either.

excerpts from my journal

every time i order a coffee for myself,
i make sure to bring my mother's order home as well.
extra-large decaf,
with two milk and one sugar.
one bag in, one on the side.

and i wonder if it reminds her
of when my father
used to bring it home for her after work.
i wonder if i ever help her remember him fondly.

on my drives to the gym,
the one i complain about being twenty minutes too long,
some days, i appreciate the distance.
my subjective excuse
to hum the songs my first love once played
on quiet drives home.

i laugh like my childhood best friend—
loud, full, unapologetic.
a sound i inherited without meaning to.

we are collections of the people we have loved,
for the good and the bad.
and perhaps this is what allows us
to remember them in ways
that do not feel like haunting,
just a quiet linger.

i still prefer my sandwiches cut into triangles,
though my grandmother
is no longer able to make them for me.
but the crust no longer bothers me.

sarai nichole

i still flinch at a song i swore i had forgotten,
but i belt out each lyric proudly,
as if i can still hear their voices beside me.

i don't think love ever quite disappears—
it simply reshapes itself
into something we can bear.

it lingers in the way we speak,
in the way we move,
in the way both our eyes fade into the distance
when lost in thought.

and it makes me wonder—

who still hums the song i once overplayed?
who still hears my voice
when they say a certain word?

do we ever really leave the people who loved us?

we are museums of love,
and we have created exhibits
out of what was once too hard to swallow.

a quiet way of saying:

"i will always love the version of you that loved me too."

excerpts from my journal

i know i have more than one purpose.
some are loud,
some are soft,
some are still waiting for me.

but i do not need to name them
to know they are mine.

i just want my own kitchen,
where the windows stay open
in the summer,
and the smell of vanilla and citrus
lives in the walls.

i want two golden retrievers,
all sun and speed,
bouncing through fields too wide to hold them.

i want to wake up early enough
to see the mist settle over the countryside,
to make my coffee slow,
to read poetry out loud to no one but myself.

sarai nichole

i want to know every poem by heart.
to live inside words
i did not write,
but wish i had.

i want twins someday,
so that someone i love
will always have someone to love them back.

i want to study forensic psychology—
to honour stories written in evidence,
not words.

i want to be kissed in the rain.
to stand there and let it happen,
without rushing inside,
without worrying about the cold.

my dreams may not be big enough to change the world,

but they are big enough to change mine.

ACKNOWLEDGEMENTS

First and foremost, **THANK YOU. THANK YOU. THANK YOU!!!**

This book would not exist without the love, patience, and support of so many people. To my family, thank you for your unwavering belief in me, even on the days I doubted myself. To my friends who listened, read my drafts, and encouraged me to keep writing—your words have meant everything.

A special thank you to my mom—for reading every single draft I sent your way (and believe me, I sent them all!), even on your busiest days, especially then. Thank you for teaching me, from a young age, that I could do anything I put my mind to. You are my greatest muse, my deepest inspiration, and I hope I made you proud.

To Victoria Noon, my best friend—thank you for being my very first reader, for your insights, and for reminding me that poetry is meant to be shared. Thank you for being my safe space, and the greatest friend a girl could ask for. Without you, this book would have never come into existence, and for that, I will never be able to thank you enough.

To Janet Murray, who taught me the power of being able to forgive without repression. Thank you for encouraging me to find my voice and let it be heard.

To Joshua Macleod, thank you for editing my work on sleepless nights and for supporting me from the very start—when my words were merely dreams.

To my dearest friends, those honored within these pages and those who were not—thank you for being a part of this journey we call life. Thank you for holding my hand, for trusting me with our shared stories, for allowing me to put into words the moments we will never forget—ones that can never be unwritten, both figuratively and literally.

To my little sister, thank you for always being proud of me. May my words remind you that you will never be alone in this world, that I will always be within arm's reach.

sarai nichole

To my grandmother, thank you for being my second home. For allowing me to share some of our most cherished memories with the world, and for always being a safe space.

To my grandfather, who is no longer with me in the physical world—thank you for living on in the spaces that will always carry your weight. Thank you for existing in all my favorite people. Thank you for being the man that stayed, as long as he could. You will always live on in my heart. Until we meet again.

To my online community—every comment, share, and message from you has reminded me that words have power. You gave me the courage to put this book into the world.

And finally, to you— the person holding this book in your hands. Thank you for letting my words find you. I hope you see pieces of yourself in these pages.

With love and gratitude,
Sarai Nichole <33

About the Author

Sarai Nichole is a poet and storyteller who writes to make sense of the world around her. Through raw, unfiltered verse, she explores love, loss, healing, and the quiet moments in between. Her words serve as both a reflection of her own journey and an offering to those who find pieces of themselves in her poetry.

She believes poetry is a safe space—
a place where feelings are allowed to exist fully, without apology.

Born and raised in Bradford, Ontario, Sarai has spent years turning emotions into ink, finding solace in the art of writing. When she's not filling pages with poetry, you can find her getting lost in bookstores, battling cuteness aggression from her two beloved dogs, or sipping coffee while people-watching.

Follow her journey:

Instagram: [@sarai.nichole]

TikTok: [@sarai.nichole]

Made in the USA
Middletown, DE
07 January 2026

23992610R00124